Unleashing THE B.R.A.V.E. WITHIN

A Journal of Empowerment

by

APRIL MOODY-JENNINGS

Brave By Design:
Unleashing The Brave Within: A Journal of Empowerment

Copyright © 2023 by April Moody-Jennings

ISBN: 979-8-88962-008-2

Insyte Creative Agency, LLC
Ocoee, Florida
insytecreativeagency@aol.com

Printed in the United States of America

Published in Ocoee, Florida
Published By: Insyte Creative Agency, LL

A Note from the Author

Continuation of the Prequel "A Love Letter to A Black Woman"

Discover the triumphant journey of black women in Brave By Design: Embodying the Essence of Black Womanhood. The eagerly awaited continuation of the prequel "A Love Letter to A Black Woman." This inspiring book is part of a trilogy that includes the "Brave By Design series" and a thoughtfully crafted journal, empowering you to embrace your true self, cultivate resilience, and ignite the fire within.

Brave By Design. takes you on an awe-inspiring journey to explore the essence of being B.R.A.V.E. - Black, Resilient, Authentic, Victorious, and Empowered. A diverse tapestry of backgrounds, experiences, and aspirations binds black women together, united by a shared heritage and relentless spirit.

Embrace your unique beauty, nurture self-confidence, and unlock the potential of setting and achieving your goals. Brave By Design offers practical guidance, empowering insights, and inspiring anecdotes that will ignite the fire within your soul.

This captivating continuation is not just about personal growth; it emphasizes the power of collective unity. You'll delve into the significance of sisterhood, fostering connections, and being a guiding light for future generations. Together, black women can create a ripple effect that extends far beyond their individual lives.

As a pivotal part of a trilogy that includes "A Love Letter to A Black Woman" and "Brave By Design," this book invites you to redefine power, resilience, and victory. It is a call to action, urging all women to rise unapologetically and create a world where their voices are heard, their achievements celebrated, and their dreams boundless.

Celebrate who you are - unapologetically B.R.A.V.E. women! Brave By Design: Embodying the Essence of Black Womanhood marks the next chapter of a transformative series that empowers you to step into your greatness and leave an everlasting mark on the world.

Continue the journey of self-discovery and empowerment. Together, let's shape a world where possibilities know no limits!

Contents

Introduction

Welcome to **Brave by Design Journal!** This journal is a vibrant space for Black women to celebrate their strength, resilience, authenticity, victories, and empowerment. Embrace your journey with joy, as we explore the essence of B.R.A.V.E. and the empowering prompts that will inspire you to express your unique story fearlessly. With these diva moments and journal prompts, embrace the essence of the fearless and fabulous diva within you. Capture the brilliance, radiance, and confidence that define your journey, and let your inner star shine brightly in every aspect of your life. Keep journaling, keep dazzling, and keep being the diva who is unapologetically and authentically herself. The world is your stage, and you were born to shine!

So, what is a "Diva Moment?"

Ah, behold the glorious diva moment! Picture this: a burst of confetti raining down from the heavens, dazzling lights swirling around like a disco ball, and a soulful melody filling the air. In the spotlight, you stand tall, exuding the confidence of a thousand runway models and the charm of a Hollywood star. Your smile could light up the night sky, and your laughter is infectious, spreading like wildfire to captivate everyone around you.

With each graceful stride, you command attention like a queen reigning over her empire. Your presence is a force to be reckoned with, a magnetic pull that draws admirers near, who can't help but bask in your irresistible aura. You dance through life with a twinkle in your eye, embracing every challenge like a diva gracefully gliding through a dance routine.

When life throws lemons your way, you don't just make lemonade; you turn it into a sparkling lemon cocktail, garnished with confidence and a splash of sass. Your spirit is unbreakable, and your resilience shines like a beacon, guiding others towards their own inner power.

In your diva moment, you're the star of your own show, the heroine of your unique story. You wear your authenticity like a designer gown, adorned with sequins of self-love and pearls of wisdom. You walk with the rhythm of your heart, swaying to the beat of your dreams, and embracing every twist and turn on the path to greatness.

So, my fabulous diva, revel in your moments of brilliance, embrace your quirks, and twirl in the spotlight of your uniqueness. Your diva spirit is a gift to the world, inspiring others to embrace their own inner shine. So keep shining, keep dazzling, and keep being the fearless and fabulous diva you were born to be! Embrace your diva moments, and let the world witness the magic of your radiance!

Chapter 1

Black Beauty *and* Brilliance

> " In the tapestry of life, I am a masterpiece woven with the hues of resilience and beauty."

PROMPT 1: Reflect on your favorite qualities that make you proud of being a Black woman. Embrace your uniqueness and write down the things that make you shine.

....

....

....

....

....

....

....

Prompt 2: How do you channel your resilience and strength in times of adversity? Share experiences where you overcame challenges with courage and grace.

....

....

....

....

....

....

....

DIVA MOMENT: Embracing Your Diva Power

Describe a moment when you felt like a true diva, exuding confidence and charisma. How can you carry that powerful energy into other areas of your life?

....

....

....

....

....

....

....

....

....

List five qualities that make you a diva and celebrate how they contribute to your unique charm and allure.

....

....

....

....

....

Chapter 2

Unleashing *Your* B.R.A.V.E. Spirit

" Be bold, be resilient, be authentic, be victorious, and be empowered – unleash your inner B.R.A.V.E. spirit!

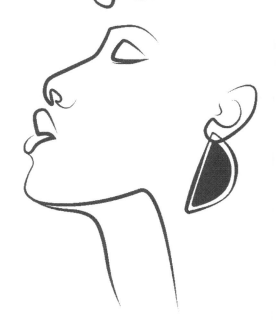

Remember, my B.R.A.V.E. divas, you are powerful, resilient, and unstoppable. When you unleash your B.R.A.V.E. spirit, you become a force of inspiration and empowerment for others. So go forth, and let your B.R.A.V.E. spirit soar high and bright, illuminating the path for others to follow. You are fierce and fabulous! it's time to unleash your B.R.A.V.E. spirit and let the world witness the extraordinary power within you!

Prompt 1: Reflect on the times you added a touch of sparkle to someone else's life. How can you keep spreading joy and positivity like the dazzling diva you are?

....

....

....

....

Prompt 2: Write about a recent achievement or accomplishment that made you feel like a shining star. How can you keep striving for greatness?

....

....

....

....

....

Be Bold and Fearless: Embrace your uniqueness and stand confidently in your truth. Don't be afraid to take risks and step outside your comfort zone. Remember, your boldest moves lead to the most extraordinary moments.

Resilience is Your Superpower: Life may throw challenges your way, but you, my resilient divas, have the strength to rise above it all. Embrace each obstacle as an opportunity to grow and thrive.

Authenticity is Your Style: Own your authentic self, unapologetically. Embrace your quirks, imperfections, and unique qualities that make you beautiful. Your authenticity radiates a captivating light that draws others in.

Victory Awaits Your Command: Believe in your ability to achieve greatness. Set bold goals and celebrate each victory, no matter how big or small. Remember, every triumph adds to your unshakable spirit.

Empowerment is Your Birthright: Empower yourself and others around you. Lift each other up, encourage one another, and create a sisterhood that fosters strength and support.

Let Love Be Your Guiding Light: Approach challenges and triumphs with love and compassion. Love yourself unconditionally and share that love with others. Love is the foundation of your B.R.A.V.E. spirit.

Embrace Your Inner Diva: Pamper yourself with self-care and indulge in moments of self-love. You are worthy of all the love, care, and attention you give to others.

Radiate Confidence: Dress in a way that reflects your true self, for fashion is an expression of your radiant soul. Let your style be an outward reflection of your inner B.R.A.V.E. spirit.

Celebrate Every Step: Acknowledge every step you take on this journey. Whether it's a step forward or a step back, celebrate your growth and the lessons learned along the way.

DIVA MOMENT: Unleashing Your Inner Glitter

Reflect on the times you added a touch of sparkle to someone else's life. How can you keep spreading joy and positivity like the dazzling diva you are?

....

....

....

....

Write about a recent achievement or accomplishment that made you feel like a shining star. How can you keep striving for greatness?

....

....

....

....

Sparkle in Your Soul: Journal about the things that make your soul shine and bring out your inner glitter. What activities, passions, or experiences make you feel alive and full of joy?

....

....

....

....

Glamorous Goals: Write down three glamorous goals you want to achieve in your life. How can you infuse your unique sparkle and shine into pursuing these dreams?

....

....

....

....

....

Glowing Affirmations: Create glittery affirmations that remind you of your inner beauty and worth. Repeat them daily to boost your confidence and embrace your inner glitter.

Shimmering Self-Expression: Embrace a form of creative expression that allows you to show off your inner glitter. Whether it's through art, writing, fashion, or dance, let your sparkle shine.

Twinkling Moments of Gratitude: Reflect on moments in your life when your inner glitter sparkled the brightest. What were you doing, and how can you incorporate more of these moments into your daily life?

....

....

....

....

....

....

....

....

....

....

....

....

....

Radiant Self-Care Rituals: Design a self-care routine that adds an extra layer of glitter to your life. Treat yourself like the fabulous diva you are with pampering and love.

	M	T	W	TH	F	SA	SU
Drink a glass of water to start the day	☐	☐	☐	☐	☐	☐	☐
Enjoy 45 minutes of exercise	☐	☐	☐	☐	☐	☐	☐
Get some fresh air	☐	☐	☐	☐	☐	☐	☐
Have a healthy breakfast	☐	☐	☐	☐	☐	☐	☐
Enjoy a warm morning drink	☐	☐	☐	☐	☐	☐	☐
Plan out your day in your planner	☐	☐	☐	☐	☐	☐	☐
Stretch your body	☐	☐	☐	☐	☐	☐	☐
Take regular breaks	☐	☐	☐	☐	☐	☐	☐
Enjoy some sunshine	☐	☐	☐	☐	☐	☐	☐
Take hot/Cold bath or shower	☐	☐	☐	☐	☐	☐	☐
Read something meaningful	☐	☐	☐	☐	☐	☐	☐
Play some invigorating music	☐	☐	☐	☐	☐	☐	☐
Disconnect	☐	☐	☐	☐	☐	☐	☐
Eat a healthy snack	☐	☐	☐	☐	☐	☐	☐
Wind down by avoiding bright light at night	☐	☐	☐	☐	☐	☐	☐
Get in bed before 10pm	☐	☐	☐	☐	☐	☐	☐

Confidence, Glitter, Repeat: Write a mantra that incorporates the words "confidence" and "glitter." Repeat it whenever you need a boost of self-assurance and empowerment.

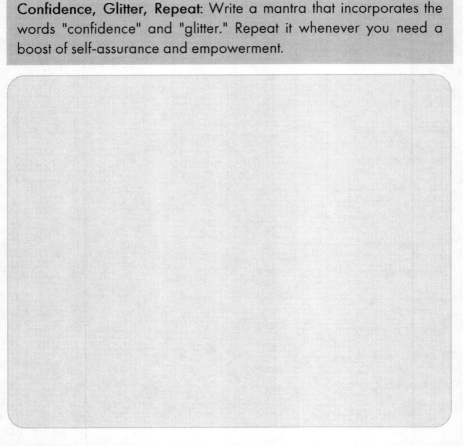

Sparkle Fashion Inspiration: Explore fashion styles and accessories that add sparkle and glitter to your outfits. Use your "Brave By Design" Journal about how incorporating these elements makes you feel.

Shine in Sisterhood: Celebrate the fabulous women in your life who also radiate their inner glitter. Write about how your sisterhood of glittering souls empowers and supports each other.

Unleash Your Glitter Goals: Create a vision board filled with images that represent your goals and aspirations. Use glitter pens or stickers to add extra sparkle to your dreams.

Confetti of Joy: Journal about moments of pure joy in your life, both big and small. How can you create more of these confetti-filled moments to spread glitter in your everyday life?

A Glittery Legacy: Write a letter to your future self, reminding her of the vibrant and dazzling woman she is. Share words of encouragement and sprinkle some extra glittery wisdom

....

....

....

....

....

....

....

....

....

Glowing Reflection: Look back at your journal entries and celebrate the growth and transformation of your inner glitter. Acknowledge the strength and resilience you've discovered along the way.

Embrace your inner glitter, my sparkling divas, and let it shine brightly in every aspect of your life. Embrace the joy, confidence, and beauty that comes from unleashing your glittery spirit. Your inner sparkle is a gift to be cherished and shared with the world. So go forth and dazzle the world with your radiant presence, for you are a shimmering testament to the power of inner glitter!

Chapter 3

Resilience *and* Radiance

" True beauty emanates from within, where resilience and self-love dance in harmony."

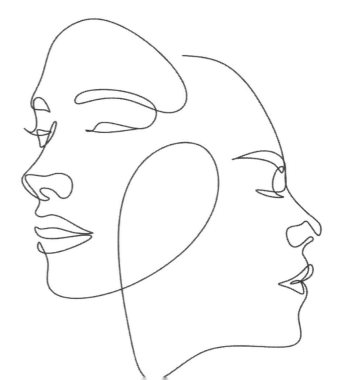

Prompt 1: Recall a significant triumph or accomplishment that made you feel victorious. Describe the journey leading to that moment and the lessons you learned along the way.

Prompt 2: Write about the support system that helped you thrive during challenging times. Express gratitude to those who have been part of your victories

Journal Prompts for Embracing Resilience, Radiance, and Owning Your Style:

Resilience Reflection: Journal about a challenging situation you've overcome and how it has made you stronger and more resilient. How can you use this experience as a source of inspiration in your life?

....

....

....

....

....

....

....

....

....

....

Radiant Moments: Write about moments when you felt the most radiant and confident. What were you doing, and what elements of your style contributed to your radiance?

....

....

....

....

....

....

....

....

Fashion Freedom: Describe a fashion item or style that you've always admired but haven't tried yet. What's holding you back? Write about how embracing this new style could empower you.

....

....

....

....

....

....

....

....

Resilient Role Model: Reflect on a person you admire for their resilience. What qualities do they possess that inspire you to navigate life's challenges with grace?

....

....

....

....

....

....

....

Radiant Self-Care Routine: Create a self-care routine that enhances your radiance. Incorporate elements like skincare, makeup, or relaxation practices that make you feel radiant from within.

....

....

....

....

....

....

....

Fashion Exploration: Experiment with a new fashion trend or accessory that intrigues you. Journal about your experience and how it aligns with your personal style.

....

....

....

....

....

....

....

....

Resilience in Adversity: Write about a time when your resilience helped you push through a difficult period in your life. How did you maintain a positive outlook during challenging times?

....

....

....

....

....

....

....

....

Radiant Affirmations: Create affirmations that celebrate your radiant energy and inner beauty. Repeat them daily to boost your confidence and embrace your unique radiance.

Style Confidence Boosters: List five fashion pieces or accessories that make you feel like a diva. Why do these items boost your confidence, and how can you incorporate them into your daily style.

Resilience in Fashion: Share a story about how fashion has been a source of resilience in your life. Maybe a favorite outfit helped you through a tough moment or gave you the confidence to conquer a challenge.

....

....

....

....

....

....

....

Radiant Body Positivity: Write about the parts of your body that you love and celebrate them as unique features that make you beautiful. Embrace body positivity in your radiant diva style.

....

....

....

....

....

....

....

Style and Empowerment: Journal about how owning your style and fashion choices has contributed to feeling empowered and confident in various aspects of your life.

....

....

....

....

....

....

Resilience Vision Board: Create a vision board that represents your vision of resilience, radiance, and fashion goals. Use images and words that inspire you to embrace your true self unapologetically.

My resilient, radiant, and stylish diva, you have the power to embrace resilience, radiance, and your unique fashion sense. Through your authentic expression, you become a beacon of resilience, radiance, and fierce style. Let your inner diva shine brilliantly in every facet of your life!

DIVA MOMENT 2: Owning Your Style and Fashion

Create a fashion vision board that reflects your fabulous sense of style. What trends, colors, and accessories make you feel like the ultimate diva?

Prompts, Reminders, Suggestions, and Advice:

Style Story: Reflect on the evolution of your personal style over the years. Journal about the moments and experiences that have shaped your unique fashion journey.

Signature Diva Look: Describe your signature diva look that makes you feel confident and empowered. Whether it's a bold accessory or a favorite outfit, celebrate the elements that define your style.

Fashion Fantasy: Imagine you're a fashion designer creating your dream clothing line. Draw or describe the pieces that would represent your authentic style as a diva.

Fashion Icon Inspiration: Choose a fashion icon who inspires you, and journal about the elements of their style that resonate with your own. How can you incorporate those inspirations into your wardrobe?

....

....

....

....

....

....

....

....

Diva Dress-Up Play: Set aside some time for a dress-up playdate with your wardrobe. Mix and match different pieces to create fun and unexpected outfit combinations that express your true diva style.

Style Savvy Tips: Write a list of fashion tips and tricks that help you feel stylish and confident every day. Share your style secrets with your future self as a reminder of your unique style wisdom.

Style Comfort Zone Stretch: Challenge yourself to step outside your style comfort zone. Try on clothing or accessories that you wouldn't typically wear and journal about the experience.

Thrift Store Treasures: Visit a thrift store and hunt for hidden fashion treasures that align with your diva style. Share the excitement of finding unique pieces at a great value.

Diva Style Confidence Boosters: Write down three things you love most about your style and celebrate these confidence-boosting elements that make you shine as a diva.

Celebrate your unique fashion sense and know that you are a diva who owns her style with grace and flair. Your style journey is a masterpiece in progress, and through your authentic expression, you paint the world with your signature style. Embrace your inner diva, and let her shine brightly in every fashion choice you make!

Resilience and Radiance:

Resilient Diva Tales: Share a story of a time when your resilience shone through in a challenging situation. Reflect on how you overcame adversity with your radiant spirit, and celebrate your triumph!

Radiant Self-Care Rituals: Create a list of self-care rituals that make you feel radiant and rejuvenated. From spa days to dancing in your living room, embrace self-care as a powerful tool for resilience.

Divine Resilience Playlist: Design a playlist of uplifting songs that boost your resilience and radiance. Play it loud and proud, and let the music inspire your inner diva warrior!

Resilient Rebirth: Describe a moment of transformation when you emerged stronger and more radiant after overcoming a difficult situation. Embrace your resilience as a force that leads to growth and renewal.

Radiant Affirmations: Write affirmations that remind you of your resilience and radiance. Repeat them with confidence, knowing that you are a diva who can handle anything life throws your way.

Divine Comedy Hour: Share a funny or lighthearted story that showcases how you've embraced humor in tough times. Laughter is a powerful tool for a radiant and resilient diva!

Resilience Vision Board: Create a vision board that represents your vision of resilience and radiance. Use images and words that inspire and motivate you to stay strong and shine brightly.

Radiant Growth Journal: Journal about the ways you've grown and evolved through challenges. Embrace the lessons learned and celebrate the resilience that led to your radiant growth.

Resilient Superpowers: Imagine you have superhero powers of resilience and radiance. Describe your unique abilities and how you would use them to overcome any obstacle like a true diva warrior.

Radiant Dance Party: Host a solo dance party, celebrating your resilience and radiance. Move your body with freedom and joy, knowing that you are a diva who dances through life's ups and downs.

Remember, my resilient and radiant diva, you have the strength to overcome any challenge and the radiance to shine brightly through it all. Embrace these journal prompts with a smile, celebrating your resilience and knowing that you are a diva who radiates strength and joy. You are a force of resilience and radiance, and through your inner diva's light, you illuminate the world around you. Embrace your inner diva, and let her bask in the spotlight of resilience and radiance!

Chapter 4

Embracing
Authenticity

❝In a world craving authenticity, I choose to stand tall, embracing my unique self with pride."

Prompt: Discovering My Authentic Self: Journal about a moment in your life when you felt truly authentic and genuine. What circumstances or experiences allowed you to be your true self, and how did it feel to embrace your authenticity?

....

....

....

....

....

....

Prompt: Unapologetically Me: Reflect on times when you may have hidden or suppressed aspects of your true self to please others or fit in. Write about the importance of embracing your authentic self and the freedom that comes with being unapologetically you.

....

....

....

....

....

....

Prompt: Authenticity in Relationships: Explore how authenticity plays a role in your relationships with others. Have you ever experienced the power of being authentic with someone, and how did it impact the connection and trust between you?

....

....

....

....

....

....

....

Prompt: Letting Go of Expectations: Journal about the pressure to conform to societal or cultural expectations and how it can hinder your authentic expression. Share your journey of releasing these expectations and embracing your unique identity.

....

....

....

....

....

....

....

Prompt: Embracing Flaws and Imperfections: Embrace your authentic self by acknowledging and accepting your flaws and imperfections. Write about how embracing these aspects of yourself has led to personal growth and a greater sense of self-love.

DIVA MOMENT: Prompts, Reminders, Suggestions, and Advice:

Authentic Style Icon: Imagine your authentic self as a style icon. Describe the fabulous outfits and accessories that represent your true essence. Have fun designing your signature look!

Authenticity Playlist: Create a playlist of songs that celebrate individuality and authenticity. Dance and sing along like a true diva who is unafraid to show the world her unique self!

Embracing Quirks: Journal about your quirkiest habits or interests that make you authentically you. Celebrate these quirks as the special traits that set you apart in the most delightful way.

Authentic Adventures: Write a "bucket list" of authentic adventures you'd love to experience as your true self. Whether it's trying a new hobby or embarking on a solo journey, let your authentic spirit guide your choices.

....

....

....

....

....

....

....

Authentic Tribe: Imagine a tribe of authentic divas who support and celebrate each other's uniqueness. Describe the qualities of your dream tribe, and how you can create a circle of empowering connections.

....
....
....
....
....
....
....

Authentic Wisdom: Reflect on the wisdom that comes from being authentic. Write down your own life lessons and share the insights you've gained from embracing your authentic self.

....
....
....
....
....
....
....

Authentic Laugh-Out-Loud: Share a funny story or memory that showcases your authenticity. Laughter is the best accessory for any diva who owns her uniqueness!

....

....

....

....

....

....

....

....

Authentic Affirmations: Create a collection of affirmations that celebrate your authentic self. Repeat them daily to boost your confidence and embrace your true diva essence.

....

....

....

....

....

....

....

....

Authentic Vision Board: Design a vision board that reflects your authentic dreams and aspirations. Use images, words, and symbols that represent your true desires and intentions.

Authentic Signature Move: Invent a fabulous signature move that embodies your authenticity. It could be a dance move, a hand gesture, or anything that makes you feel like a diva who is confidently herself.

Remember, my authentic diva, embracing your true self is a journey of self-discovery and celebration. Embrace these journal prompts with joy and enthusiasm, celebrating your uniqueness and knowing that you are a diva who shines brightly by being authentically you. You are a diva who knows how to radiate authenticity and show the world your true essence. Embrace your inner diva, and let her bask in the spotlight of genuine self-expression and self-love! Embrace these journal prompts with honesty and vulnerability, celebrating your authentic self and knowing that you are a diva who radiates genuine beauty and strength. You are uniquely and wonderfully you, and through your authenticity, you shine brighter than ever before. Embrace your inner diva, and let her bask in the light of authenticity and self-acceptance

Chapter 5

Victorious and Unstoppable

> "Victory awaits those who dare to dream, who dare to believe, and who dare to persevere."

My Proudest Moment: Reflect on a recent accomplishment or achievement that made you feel victorious and empowered. Describe the experience, the challenges you overcame, and the emotions that accompanied your success.

....

....

....

....

....

....

Diva Mantras: Create a list of empowering mantras that remind you of your strength and power. Write them down and repeat them daily to cultivate a sense of empowerment and victory.

....

....

....

....

....

....

....

Celebrating My Inner Champion: Imagine you're hosting a celebration in honor of your inner champion. Journal about the guest list, decorations, and activities you would have to honor the victorious and empowered diva within you.

....

....

....

....

....

....

....

Defying Limitations: Journal about a time when you defied societal or personal limitations and proved to yourself and others that you are capable of greatness. How did this experience make you feel empowered and unstoppable?

....

....

....

....

....

....

....

Empowering Visualization: Take a few moments to close your eyes and visualize yourself achieving a significant goal or dream. Imagine every detail of your victorious moment, including the emotions and sense of empowerment that come with it. Describe this visualization in your journal, and allow it to fuel your motivation and determination.

Remember, my victorious and empowered diva, you possess the strength and power to conquer any challenge that comes your way. Embrace these journal prompts with joy and enthusiasm, celebrating your victories and knowing that you are a force to be reckoned with. You are a diva who knows how to claim her power and shine brightly in the world. Embrace your inner champion and let her bask in the glory of victory and empowerment!

DIVA MOMENT: Empowered in the Spotlight

Recall a moment when you took center stage and dazzled everyone around you. How did it feel to be the star of the show?

....

....

....

....

....

....

....

....

Reflect on any challenges you faced in the spotlight and how you overcame them with grace and tenacity.

....

....

....

....

....

....

....

Diva Moment Description:

Welcome to the diva victory celebration, where you stand tall as the victorious and unstoppable force that you are! Imagine confetti flying and applause filling the room as you embrace your triumphs and set your sights on conquering new heights. Each prompt encourages you to relish in laughter, positivity, and the unstoppable spirit of a diva who knows she can achieve anything!

Prompts, Reminders, Suggestions, and Advice:

Victorious Victory Dance: Create your signature victory dance, complete with sassy moves and a winning attitude. Dance like nobody's watching, and let your diva spirit shine!

Celebration Playlist: Craft a celebration playlist filled with songs that make you feel victorious and unstoppable. Play it on full blast and dance like a diva who has just conquered the world!

Champion's Pep Talk: Write yourself a champion's pep talk, empowering yourself to overcome any obstacle with confidence and determination. Read it aloud with diva flair whenever you need a boost!

Unstoppable Affirmations: Invent affirmations that embrace your unstoppable nature. Repeat them throughout the day like a diva on a mission to greatness!

Diva Victory March: Take a victory march around your living space or neighborhood. Stride like a diva on a runway, savoring the feeling of success with every step.

Victory Journal: Create a "Victory Journal" where you document your achievements and triumphs, big and small. Relive the moments that make you feel invincible like a diva with a crown!

Celebrate Each Step: Celebrate every little step you take towards your goals. Each achievement, no matter how small, is a diva-worthy accomplishment!

Power Pose Practice: Practice power poses that make you feel victorious and confident. Stand tall like a diva superstar, ready to take on the world!

Confetti of Success: Design your own confetti of success with positive words and symbols. Sprinkle it around your space, embracing the energy of triumph like a diva on a red carpet!

Unstoppable Vision Board: Create an unstoppable vision board filled with images that represent your dreams and aspirations. Let it remind you that you're a diva on a journey to greatness!

Remember, my unstoppable diva, victory is your divine birthright, and nothing can stand in your way. Embrace these diva moments with laughter and enthusiasm, celebrating every success along the way. You are a diva who knows how to conquer and achieve, and through your unstoppable spirit, you shine brighter than ever before. Embrace your inner diva and let her bask in the spotlight of victory and triumph!

Chapter 6

Sisterhood *and* Support

> ❝Sisterhood is a sacred bond, where we lift each other higher and champion one another's dreams."

Express gratitude for the people and experiences that have contributed to your growth and journey. What lessons are you most grateful for?

....

....

....

....

....

....

....

Reflect on your growth as a BB.R.A.V.E. woman. How have you evolved, and what are you most proud of in your journey?

....

....

....

....

....

....

....

DIVA MOMENT: Embracing Sisterhood

Reflect on a cherished sisterhood moment that brought joy and strength to your life. How can you nurture these connections and spread positivity within your sisterhood circle?

....

....

....

....

....

....

....

Write a letter of appreciation to a fellow diva who has been a pillar of support and empowerment in your life.

....

....

....

....

....

....

....

Reflect on the strong women who have been part of your life's journey. Write down the qualities that inspire you and how they have impacted your life.

....
....
....
....
....
....
....
....
....
....
....
....
....
....
....

Join the B.R.A.V.E facebook group!

DIVA MOMENT: Embracing Sisterhood

Write a love letter to your sisterhood, expressing gratitude for their unwavering support and fabulousness.

....

....

....

....

....

....

....

....

....

....

....

....

....

....

....

Reminder: When divas come together, magic happens! Celebrate the sisterhood that lifts you higher!

Chapter 7

Stress Management *and* Inner Peace

❝ You can never tell which way
the wind is blowing until the
wind blows." - HENRY DAVID THOREAU

Create a list of daily stress-relief activities that help you unwind and find inner peace. How can you incorporate at least one of these activities into your daily routine?

....

....

....

....

....

....

....

Reflect on the moments when you feel most stressed. What are some effective ways to cope with stress and bring yourself back to a place of calm?

....

....

....

....

....

....

....

DIVA MOMENT: Diva Moment Description:

Imagine yourself in a serene garden, surrounded by colorful butterflies fluttering around. Soft music plays in the background, and you feel a gentle breeze caressing your face. With a cup of herbal tea in hand, you take a deep breath, exhaling all worries and stress. Your diva spirit is at ease, embracing the art of relaxation with poise and grace.

Prompts, Reminders, Suggestions, and Advice:

Diva Serenity Soiree: Host a mini spa day at home, complete with face masks, scented candles, and soothing music. Embrace the diva within as you pamper yourself like the queen you are!

Divinely Delicious Laughter: Call a friend or watch a hilarious comedy to have a good laugh. Laughter is a diva's secret weapon against stress!

Crown Your Priorities: Remember, you're the CEO of your life. Crown your priorities with grace, diva, and delegate the rest to maintain your inner peace.

Diva Retreat Time: Designate a special space in your home as your diva retreat, where you can meditate, journal, or simply relax and rejuvenate.

Glamorous Gratitude: Embrace the diva habit of expressing gratitude daily. List three things you're grateful for and bask in the warm glow of appreciation.

Glowing Affirmations: Create your own diva affirmations to uplift your spirit and remind yourself of your inner strength.

Diva Dance Break: Whenever stress knocks on your door, put on your favorite song, and dance like nobody's watching. Let your diva spirit groove away the worries!

Curtain Call Breathing: Practice deep breathing exercises like a diva preparing for her grand entrance. Inhale confidence, exhale stress.

Celestial Sleep Ritual: Create a soothing bedtime ritual to ensure a restful sleep. Sprinkle your bed with positivity and lay your head down like the sleeping beauty you are.

Divine Detox: Detox your mind from negative thoughts and toxic energy. Surround yourself with positivity, and release what no longer serves your diva journey.

Remember, my radiant diva, you hold the power to manage stress with elegance and inner peace. Embrace these fun-filled moments and let your diva spirit guide you towards a life filled with serenity and joy. Dance through life with grace and ease, for you are the star of your own dazzling show!

Chapter 8

Sparkling *in* *the* Spotlight

" Center stage is my canvas, and I paint a masterpiece of brilliance and charm with every step."

Reflect on a time when you shone in the spotlight, captivating an audience. How can you continue to sparkle in your endeavors?

....

....

....

....

....

....

....

Write about a challenge you faced while in the spotlight and how you transformed it into an opportunity to dazzle.

....

....

....

....

....

....

....

....

Write a love letter to yourself, embracing all your strengths, uniqueness, and beauty. How can you practice self-love on a daily basis?

....

....

....

....

....

....

....

Recall a moment when you felt particularly confident and proud of yourself. How can you carry that feeling of confidence into other areas of your life?

....

....

....

....

....

....

....

DIVA MOMENT: Diva Moment Description:

Step into a delightful diva spa, where self-love is the theme of the day. Surrounded by scented candles and soothing music, you embark on a journey of self-discovery and self-adoration. Each prompt encourages you to embrace your inner diva with laughter, love, and a touch of whimsy. As you journal, your heart brims with self-compassion and a newfound appreciation for the incredible woman you are!

Prompts, Reminders, Suggestions, and Advice:

Self-Love Letter: Write a love letter to yourself, showering compliments and affirmations like confetti. Let your inner diva pen a heartfelt ode to the amazing person you see in the mirror.

Diva Dance Break: Take a diva dance break, swaying to your favorite empowering songs. Embrace your body with every move, appreciating the strength and beauty it holds.

Pamper Me Pledge: Create a "Pamper Me Pledge" where you promise to prioritize self-care. Declare this with a diva flair, and remember to indulge yourself often!

Mirror Magic Moments: Stand in front of the mirror and share the silliest jokes and funniest stories with your reflection. Let laughter be your mirror's best accessory!

Diva Affirmation Mirror: Decorate your mirror with empowering affirmations that boost your self-love. Greet yourself every day with a diva mantra that inspires greatness within.

Celebrating Inner Diva: Make a list of your unique qualities and accomplishments, and imagine throwing a grand celebration in honor of your inner diva. Party like it's your birthday!

Self-Love Haikus: Write haikus that express your journey of self-love and growth. Keep them short, sweet, and full of diva charm!

Empowering Selfies: Take a series of empowering selfies, capturing the essence of your beautiful soul. Caption each photo with a diva-inspired message of self-love.

Daily Diva Mirror Talk: Practice positive mirror talk every morning. Compliment your reflection as if you're getting ready for a glamorous red carpet event!

Gratitude & Self-Love Collage: Create a gratitude and self-love collage. Combine images that represent things you love about yourself and moments you're grateful for. Let your diva heart guide the creative process!

Remember, my fabulous diva, self-love is a divine gift you give yourself every day. Embrace these diva moments with laughter and kindness, appreciating the wonderful person you are. You are a diva who radiates self-compassion, and through this love, you shine brighter than ever before. Celebrate your unique beauty, and know that you are a magnificent force of love and empowerment in this world. Embrace your inner diva, and let her dance with joy in the spotlight of self-love!

Chapter 9

Glamourous Self-Care *Rituals*

"In the art of self-care, I pamper my mind, body, and soul, embracing the essence of relaxation and rejuvenation."

Create a list of glamorous self-care rituals that make you feel like a star. How can you incorporate these rituals into your routine?

Describe a moment when you practiced self-care and felt like the ultimate diva. How can you make self-care an indispensable part of your lifestyle?

....

....

....

....

....

....

List your accomplishments and achievements, no matter how big or small. Celebrate your growth and remind yourself of your capabilities.

....

....

....

....

....

....

Challenge negative self-talk. Write down affirmations that boost your self-esteem and repeat them daily to reinforce a positive mindset.

....

....

....

....

....

....

....

Treat yourself like the star you are with a luxurious self-care day. Diva mode: ON!

Reminder: Self-care is not selfish; it's the key to keeping your inner diva beaming and ready to take on the world!

DIVA MOMENT

Describe your ultimate self-care routine that nourishes your mind, body, and soul. How can you prioritize self-care as an essential part of your diva lifestyle?

Write about a moment when you pampered yourself and felt like a glamorous diva on cloud nine. How can you make self-care a regular ritual?

Diva Moment Description:

Welcome to the diva self-care sanctuary, where pampering and self-love are the order of the day. Picture yourself surrounded by fluffy robes, scented oils, and soothing melodies as you dive into a world of self-care bliss. Each prompt invites you to indulge in laughter, relaxation, and the joys of taking care of yourself like the fabulous diva you are!

Prompts, Reminders, Suggestions, and Advice:

Diva's Delightful Spa: Design your dream spa day, complete with luxurious treatments fit for a diva. Whether it's a bubble bath with rose petals or a DIY face mask, savor every moment of your self-care indulgence.

Laughing Yoga: Try a laughing yoga session, where you giggle your way to relaxation. Embrace the silliness and let your inner diva release all the stress through laughter!

Self-Care Bucket List: Create a self-care bucket list filled with activities that make your heart dance with joy. From reading a favorite book to going on a solo adventure, cherish each item on your list like a diva on a mission!

Diva's Day Off: Plan a diva's day off, where you take a break from responsibilities and do only things that make you happy. Your only task is to enjoy the day to the fullest!

Dance & Detox: Combine dance and detox with a diva-inspired dance workout. Move your body to your favorite tunes, and imagine releasing any negative energy with each twirl and sway.

Sassy Self-Care Mantras: Invent sassy self-care mantras that make you laugh and feel empowered. Repeat them throughout the day, embracing the diva within!

Comfy Couture: Wear your comfiest couture – fuzzy socks, oversized sweaters, or anything that makes you feel like a cozy diva. Treat yourself to a day of comfort and relaxation!

Divine Dessert Time: Create a special self-care dessert that pleases your taste buds and soothes your soul. Savor every bite like a diva indulging in her favorite delicacy.

Comedy Show Therapy: Watch a stand-up comedy show or a hilarious movie that tickles your funny bone. Laughter is the ultimate self-care medicine!

Gratitude & Self-Care Journal: Combine gratitude and self-care in a special journal. Each day, write about the self-care activities that brought you joy and the things you're grateful for. Your diva heart will glow with appreciation!

Remember, my fabulous diva, self-care is an act of love that you deserve to experience every day. Embrace these diva moments with laughter and kindness, cherishing the incredible person you are. You are a diva who knows the value of self-nurture, and through self-care, you shine brighter than ever before. Celebrate your inner diva, and let her bask in the spotlight of self-love and care!

Chapter 10

Navigating Relationships and Love as a Black Woman: *Embracing Healthy Relationships*

" I deserve healthy and fulfilling relationships. I attract love, respect, and peace.

The Diva's Love Language: Reflect on your love language and how it aligns with your partner's. How can you both embrace each other's love languages to strengthen your bond and create a harmonious relationship?

....

....

....

....

....

....

Boundaries Like a Boss: Explore the boundaries you've set in your relationships, whether it's with a partner, friends, or family. How do these boundaries empower you to prioritize your well-being and happiness?

....

....

....

....

....

....

Squad Goals for Love: Celebrate the uplifting and supportive friendships in your life. Journal about the positive influence these diva friends have on your relationships and how they inspire you to nurture healthy connections.

Sparkling Communication Gems: Describe a recent conversation with your partner that left you feeling heard, loved, and valued. How can you continue to communicate openly and honestly to build trust and understanding?

....

....

....

....

....

Diva's Dream Date: Fantasize about your dream date with a partner, filled with laughter, adventure, and love. What special moments do you envision sharing together, and how can you make some of these dreams a reality?

....

....

....

....

....

DIVA MOMENT Description: Moments of Triumph and Overcoming Relationship Challenges

You find yourself standing tall, surrounded by a team of fierce divas. Armed with love and support, you face relationship challenges head-on, like a squad of warriors ready to conquer anything. Each step you take radiates confidence, and with every stride, you leave a trail of sparkles, showing that you won't let anything dim your shine!

Prompts, Reminders, Suggestions, and Advice:

Diva Love Language: Discover your unique diva love language and communicate it with flair to your partner. Let them know how you feel loved and cherished!

Fabulous Forgiveness: Embrace your diva power to forgive, releasing negative energy and making room for love and healing.

Diva Communication Dance: Practice open and honest communication with your partner, twirling through conversations with grace and understanding.

Glamorous Boundaries: Set glamorous boundaries like a superstar diva, ensuring that your needs are respected and honored.

Diva Daredevil Date: Surprise your partner with a daring and adventurous date, trying something new together to strengthen your bond.

Sassy Self-Confidence: Remind yourself daily of your worth and diva essence. Walk through relationship challenges with the poise of a superstar!

Sparkling Compromises: Shine in the art of compromise, finding a dazzling middle ground that fosters growth in your relationship.

Diva Love Letters: Write love letters to yourself and your partner, expressing your deepest feelings with a touch of drama and heartfelt sincerity.

Glowing Gratitude Gesture: Show appreciation for your partner in a fabulous way, expressing gratitude for the little things they do.

Diva Date Night-In: Host a diva-style date night at home, complete with fancy attire, a gourmet meal, and a dance under the stars (or disco lights)!

Remember, my fierce and fabulous diva, you are the leading lady of your love story. Embrace these diva moments to conquer relationship challenges with love, compassion, and a whole lot of sparkle. In the face of adversity, dance through the obstacles with confidence, for you are the diva of your heart's desires! Celebrate your growth and triumphs, and let your relationship flourish like a true love ballad!

As you navigate the path of love, let your diva spirit guide you, and always remember that a heart full of love is a heart full of happiness! Let the love you share with your partner be as vibrant and enchanting as the sunrise, sparking endless laughter and beautiful memories. Your diva journey of love is your very own fairytale, and you're the star of this grand romance!

Chapter 11

Radiating Confidence and Empowerment

> " Confidence is my crown, and I wear it with unshakable poise, inspiring others to embrace their own royalty."

Share a moment when you felt your confidence radiating, positively impacting those around you. How can you be a guiding light for others to embrace their self-assuredness?

Describe how you overcame self-doubt and fear, stepping into your power as a fearless diva.

Diva Power Unleashed: Reflect on a moment in your life when you felt the most empowered and confident. What factors contributed to that feeling, and how can you harness that energy to empower yourself in other areas of your life?

....

....

....

....

Embracing Your Inner Diva: Journal about the qualities that make you a unique and powerful diva. How can you celebrate and embrace these qualities to boost your confidence and empower yourself?

....

....

....

....

Diva Declarations: Write a list of empowering affirmations that resonate with you. Repeat them daily, letting your inner diva know that you are capable, worthy, and deserving of greatness.

....

....

....

....

....

....

Overcoming Obstacles: Share a challenging experience you've faced, how you navigated through it, and how it contributed to your growth and empowerment. What lessons can you draw from this experience to empower yourself in the future?

....

....

....

....

....

....

....

Diva Circle of Support: Identify the people in your life who have been your biggest supporters and cheerleaders. Journal about the impact they've had on your confidence and empowerment journey, and express gratitude for their presence in your life.

....

....

....

....

....

....

....

DIVA MOMENT: Diva Moment Description:

Imagine yourself on a grand stage, spotlight shining down on you. With a dazzling smile, you strike a power pose, exuding the confidence of a diva about to deliver a show-stopping performance. Your squad of supportive divas cheer you on, knowing you're about to conquer the world with your fierce spirit and unwavering empowerment.

Prompts, Reminders, Suggestions, and Advice:

Diva Power Playlist: Create a playlist of empowering songs that make you feel like the queen of the world. Play it whenever you need a boost of confidence!

Sparkling Affirmations: Write down empowering affirmations that highlight your strengths and uniqueness. Let them be your daily reminders of how amazing you truly are.

Diva Fashion Show: Try on different outfits that make you feel confident and empowered. Strut your stuff like a diva on the runway!

Glowing Goal-Getter: Set bold and audacious goals for yourself. Embrace your diva spirit as you fearlessly chase after your dreams.

Squad of Cheerleaders: Surround yourself with a squad of empowering divas who lift you up and celebrate your achievements.

Confidence Catwalk: Practice walking with confidence and poise. Picture yourself as a diva strutting down the catwalk, owning every step you take.

Fearless Public Speaking: Join a public speaking group or practice speaking in front of a mirror. Embrace your inner diva orator and speak with charisma and conviction.

Diva Mantra Dance: Create a fun and energetic dance routine to your favorite diva mantra. Dance like nobody's watching, and feel the power within!

Diva Vision Board: Craft a vision board filled with your dreams and aspirations. Let it be a visual representation of your empowered future.

Crown of Confidence: Imagine yourself wearing a sparkling crown of confidence. Embrace the diva within as you radiate self-assuredness.

In the face of adversity, remind yourself that you're a diva, and nothing can dull your sparkle!

Reminder: Challenges may come, but you've got the diva spirit to turn them into stepping stones to greatness!

Don't' forget, my fierce and fabulous diva, confidence and empowerment are your birthright. Embrace these diva moments and let your light shine brightly. Like a radiant star, you have the power to illuminate the world with your brilliance and inspire others to do the same. So, keep strutting your stuff, keep chasing your dreams, and remember that you are a force to be reckoned with. You are a diva, strong and empowered, ready to conquer anything that comes your way! Own your power, and let your diva spirit soar high!

Chapter 12

Embracing Adversity *with* Grace

Prompt: In the face of adversity, remind yourself that you're a diva, and nothing can dull your sparkle!

Reminder: Challenges may come, but you've got the diva spirit to turn them into stepping stones to greatness!

Aging with Grace: Reflect on your current beliefs and attitudes towards aging. How can you shift your perspective to see aging as a beautiful journey filled with wisdom and growth?

Self-Care through the Ages: Journal about the self-care practices you can incorporate into your life to nurture your well-being as you age gracefully. How can you prioritize self-love and self-compassion?

Legacy and Wisdom: Write about the wisdom you've gained throughout your life and the lessons you want to pass on to future generations. How can you embrace your legacy and share your valuable experiences with others?

....

....

....

....

....

....

Embracing Change: Explore your feelings about the physical changes that come with aging. How can you embrace these changes as a natural part of life's evolution and celebrate the beauty they bring?

....

....

....

....

....

....

Gratitude for the Journey: Create a gratitude list for the experiences, accomplishments, and relationships that have enriched your life thus far. How can you carry this attitude of gratitude with you as you continue to age gracefully?

....

....

....

....

....

....

....

....

....

Diva Moments of Timeless Beauty

Diva Moment Description:

Picture yourself in a glamorous diva lounge, surrounded by your fabulous friends. The room is filled with laughter and joy as you all celebrate the wisdom and beauty that comes with age. Each diva shares their hilarious stories of embracing gray hairs and swapping anti-aging tips that make you giggle like schoolgirls. With every passing year, you all bloom like fine wine, exuding confidence and grace that lights up the room!

Prompts, Reminders, Suggestions, and Advice:

Diva Time Machine: Imagine if you had a time machine to visit your younger self. Write a letter filled with sage advice and self-love. What empowering words would you tell her to embrace the journey of aging with grace?

Youthful Laughter: Recall the funniest and most heartwarming moments of your life. Embrace the power of laughter, as it keeps you forever young at heart.

Diva Beauty Tips Exchange: Host a diva beauty tips exchange with your fabulous friends. Share skincare routines, beauty hacks, and wellness practices that leave you all glowing like goddesses.

Timeless Confidence Poses: Strike a series of timeless confidence poses, inspired by your favorite divas of past and present. Embrace your unique beauty and own it like a superstar!

Legacy of Love: Write a love letter to your future self, celebrating the incredible journey you're embarking on. Share your dreams, hopes, and the love you'll continue to radiate throughout the years.

Remember, my radiant diva, aging with confidence and grace is a gift you give yourself every day. Embrace these diva moments with joy and laughter, cherishing the wisdom and beauty that each passing year brings. Embrace the diva within and let your inner light shine brighter than ever before. Like a timeless masterpiece, you age with elegance and grace, leaving a legacy of love and empowerment for generations to come. Celebrate your journey, and remember, you are a diva, always beautiful and forever young at heart!

Chapter 13

Celebrating *the* Journey

> "In every moment, I celebrate the diva I am, embracing the journey with gratitude and a heart full of joy."

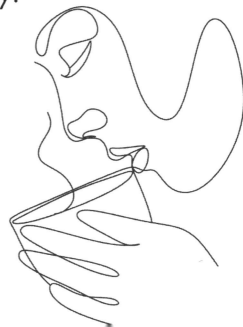

Describe the evolution of your diva journey and how you've grown and embraced your authentic self along the way.

Write about your favorite diva moment, a time when you felt fully alive and celebrated your uniqueness. How can you create more of these moments in the future?

....

....

....

....

....

....

....

....

....

....

....

....

....

Aging with Grace: Reflect on your current beliefs and attitudes towards aging. How can you shift your perspective to see aging as a beautiful journey filled with wisdom and growth?

Self-Care through the Ages: Journal about the self-care practices you can incorporate into your life to nurture your well-being as you age gracefully. How can you prioritize self-love and self-compassion?

Legacy and Wisdom: Write about the wisdom you've gained throughout your life and the lessons you want to pass on to future generations. How can you embrace your legacy and share your valuable experiences with others?

Embracing Change: Explore your feelings about the physical changes that come with aging. How can you embrace these changes as a natural part of life's evolution and celebrate the beauty they bring?

Gratitude for the Journey: Create a gratitude list for the experiences, accomplishments, and relationships that have enriched your life thus far. How can you carry this attitude of gratitude with you as you continue to age gracefully?

> Reminder: Celebrate your diva journey with a fun dance party! Move those hips, and let joy fill your heart!

DIVA MOMENT

Diva Moment Description:

Picture yourself in a glamorous diva lounge, surrounded by your fabulous friends. The room is filled with laughter and joy as you all celebrate the wisdom and beauty that comes with age. Each diva shares their hilarious stories of embracing gray hairs and swapping anti-aging tips that make you giggle like schoolgirls. With every passing year, you all bloom like fine wine, exuding confidence and grace that lights up the room!

Prompts, Reminders, Suggestions, and Advice:

Diva Time Machine: Imagine if you had a time machine to visit your younger self. Write a letter filled with sage advice and self-love. What empowering words would you tell her to embrace the journey of aging with grace?

Youthful Laughter: Recall the funniest and most heartwarming moments of your life. Embrace the power of laughter, as it keeps you forever young at heart.

Diva Beauty Tips Exchange: Host a diva beauty tips exchange with your fabulous friends. Share skincare routines, beauty hacks, and wellness practices that leave you all glowing like goddesses.

Timeless Confidence Poses: Strike a series of timeless confidence poses, inspired by your favorite divas of past and present. Embrace your unique beauty and own it like a superstar!

Legacy of Love: Write a love letter to your future self, celebrating the incredible journey you're embarking on. Share your dreams, hopes, and the love you'll continue to radiate throughout the years.

Remember, my elegant empress,, aging with confidence and grace is a gift you give yourself every day. Embrace these diva moments with joy and laughter, cherishing the wisdom and beauty that each passing year brings. Embrace the diva within and let your inner light shine brighter than ever before. Like a timeless masterpiece, you age with elegance and grace, leaving a legacy of love and empowerment for generations to come. Celebrate your journey, and remember, you are a diva, always beautiful and forever young at heart!

Chapter 14

Mindfulness *and* Meditative Practices

Divine Mindfulness: Reflect on moments when you felt deeply present and connected with your inner self. How can you incorporate more mindfulness into your daily life to cultivate a sense of divine awareness and tranquility?

....

....

....

....

....

....

Soulful Breaths: Take a few moments to close your eyes and focus on your breath. Journal about the sensations and emotions that arise during this simple act of self-care. How does focusing on your breath help you stay grounded and centered?

....

....

....

....

....

....

Gratitude Garden: Create a gratitude garden in your journal. Each day, plant seeds of gratitude by writing down three things you're grateful for. Watch your garden bloom and flourish, reminding you of the abundance in your life.

....

....

....

....

....

....

Meditative Musings: Write about your experience with meditative practices. What benefits have you noticed? How do you feel after a meditation session? Explore how meditation has positively influenced your well-being.

....

....

....

....

....

....

....

Empowered Affirmations: Craft a list of empowering affirmations that resonate with you. Use these affirmations as your daily mantras, repeating them to yourself during moments of meditation or mindfulness. How do these affirmations strengthen your sense of self and inner power?

....

....

....

....

....

....

....

DIVA MOMENTS: Inner Serenity

Diva Moment Description:

Imagine yourself in a serene diva oasis, surrounded by calming scents and soothing music. You and your diva squad are practicing mindfulness and meditation, but with a twist of laughter and joy. As you all strike your best meditation poses, someone accidentally sneezes, causing a chain reaction of giggles. Embrace the beauty of mindfulness with a touch of diva charm, finding peace and joy in every moment!

Prompts, Reminders, Suggestions, and Advice:

Diva Mindful Mornings: Design a morning routine that sets the tone for a diva day filled with mindfulness and joy. Savor each sip of your morning coffee or tea like a diva indulging in her favorite luxury.

Laughing Meditation: Experiment with laughing meditation. Gather your diva friends and have a laughter-filled meditation session, feeling your spirits lift with each joyful giggle.

Diva Zen Den: Create a diva zen den in your home, where you can escape the outside world and find tranquility amidst your favorite decor and scents.

Meditation Playlists: Curate a collection of meditation playlists featuring soothing sounds and empowering affirmations that resonate with your inner diva.

Meditation Makeover: Try meditating in different diva outfits or props, like a luxurious robe or a crown. Embrace your diva essence as you find peace within.

Gratitude Glitter Jar: Craft a gratitude glitter jar. Write down moments of gratitude on colorful pieces of paper, then sprinkle them like glitter into the jar, creating a sparkling reminder of the beauty in your life.

Diva Nature Walks: Take mindful nature walks with your diva squad, connecting with the world's beauty and finding inspiration in every flower and leaf.

Diva Breathing Exercises: Practice breathing exercises with a diva flair, inhaling confidence and exhaling any negativity.

Meditative Dance: Explore meditative dance with your friends, where you let the music guide your movements, releasing stress and embracing joy.

Affirmation Mirror Talk: Stand in front of the mirror and say empowering affirmations with your diva reflection. Watch your smile grow as you embrace the diva within.

Remember, my radiant diva, mindfulness and meditation are like sparkling gems, holding the power to enrich your life with serenity and joy. Embrace these diva moments with laughter and love, finding peace in the stillness of your heart. You are a diva with the ability to create inner harmony and to let your light shine brightly. Embrace the beauty of the present moment, and let your inner diva find peace and happiness in the midst of life's grand adventure!

Chapter 15

Finding Joy in the Little Things, *While Cultivating* a Heart of Gratitude

Simple Joys: Reflect on the little things that bring you immense joy and happiness. Write about one of these moments and how it made your heart soar with delight.

Gratitude Moments: Journal about the moments of gratitude you've experienced throughout your day. How does focusing on the small blessings enrich your life with a sense of contentment and fulfillment?

Joyful Treasures: List five things that you consider your personal joyful treasures. These can be simple objects, memories, or experiences that hold a special place in your heart.

Finding Beauty: Take a walk outdoors and immerse yourself in the beauty of nature. Write about the sights, sounds, and scents that captivate your senses and fill you with wonder.

Heartfelt Acts: Recall a time when you performed a random act of kindness or received one from someone else. Describe the warmth and joy that came from these acts, and how they touched your heart deeply.

Create a gratitude journal, jotting down at least three things you are grateful for every day. Notice how this practice shifts your perspective and brings joy.

Try something new that sparks joy in your life. Whether it's picking up a new hobby, exploring a new place, or connecting with new people, embrace the adventure.

Write a letter of appreciation to someone who has been a supportive presence in your life. Express your gratitude for their impact on your journey.

Embrace the spirit of giving back. Plan an act of kindness for someone in need and describe how this experience filled your heart with joy.

DIVA MOMENT:

Diva Moment Description:

Picture yourself in a cozy diva nook, surrounded by cushions and twinkling lights, as you embark on a journey of finding joy in the little things and cultivating a heart of gratitude. With a heart full of laughter and a sparkle in your eyes, you journal about the moments that make your soul dance and the blessings that brighten your path. Each prompt brings a smile to your face as you embrace the magic of joyful living!

Prompts, Reminders, Suggestions, and Advice:

Gratitude Laughter Diary: Start a gratitude laughter diary where you jot down the funny moments of your day. Whether it's a hilarious joke or a quirky mishap, laughter is the soul's medicine!

Divine Delights Jar: Create a "Divine Delights Jar" where you place notes of appreciation for the little things that bring you joy. Draw one out whenever you need a happiness boost!

Mirror Mirror on the Wall: Stand in front of the mirror and practice laughing at yourself! Strike your best diva pose, make silly faces, and let the mirror be your audience of joy.

Gratitude Playlist: Curate a gratitude playlist filled with uplifting and empowering songs that make you dance and sing along like a true diva.

Dance Party of Gratitude: Host a dance party of gratitude with your diva friends. Move to the rhythm of joy as you celebrate life's blessings together.

Charming Compliments: Write charming compliments for yourself in your journal. Each day, read one aloud with the flair of a diva, and watch how it boosts your self-confidence!

Gratitude Visuals: Create a collage or vision board filled with images that represent the things you're grateful for. Decorate it with sparkles and glitter to radiate diva vibes!

Joyful Journaling: Practice journaling about the little moments that bring you joy. Embrace the art of storytelling, and let your words dance on the pages like a diva on stage.

Daily Diva Dance: Start your mornings with a mini dance party! Dance like nobody's watching, and let your soul be lifted by the rhythm of happiness.

Inner Diva Declaration: Write a declaration of happiness and gratitude, embracing the little things that make your heart sing. Speak it aloud like a diva delivering her empowering speech!

Remember my sensational diva, finding joy in the little things and cultivating a heart of gratitude is your personal treasure hunt. Embrace these diva moments with laughter and love, cherishing the magic of life's smallest wonders. You are a diva who shines brightly, and through gratitude, you sparkle even more. Let your joyful spirit be your guiding light as you savor the blessings of each day. Celebrate the magic of life and know that within you lies the power to radiate joy to the world!

Made in the USA
Columbia, SC
21 October 2023

24352484R00061